MW00877696

BUNSTER DIARIES

by

H. E. DAVIS

Copyright © Hannah Elizabeth Davis 2012

All rights reserved

ISBN 978-1-291-21028-6

INTRODUCTION

This is a year in the life of Bailey Bunster, from the summer of 2011 through to the spring of 2012. Recently unearthed from its secret hiding place in the sofa, it chronicles Bailey's private thoughts about life as a house rabbit.

Despite some initial misgivings, Bailey was persuaded to publish by the offer of 42 bags (a year's supply) of dried herbs. He is now busily working on his next volume of diaries for which he has demanded an advance of 3 bananas, 12 bags of green oat hay and a tub of raisins. Negotiations are on-going but he's feeling hopeful; after all, Bunster always wins.

SUMMER

This morning while I was poking around, as you do, I found this old notebook under the oldies' bed. Once I'd dusted the years of cobwebs off it (note to self: have a word with mum about her cleaning standards) it occurred to me that I could keep a diary. Or more of a journal really. My deepest thoughts and ponderings, stuff like that.

[later] turns out my deepest thought today was about dinner. I had a lovely bit of cavolo nero this evening. That's worth noting just because it's so rare. I wish I lived in Italy instead of boring old Britain.

Need to find a good hiding place - Miss Daisy remarked on the lumpiness of the blankets in the den earlier. I did a bit of bulldozing and smoothing to cover it up but she's a smart cookie and will find it sooner or later. I don't mind so much if she reads it but she's a terrible tattle tale and will no doubt show it to the oldies. The thought of those two sniggering over my innermost thoughts is embarrassing beyond belief.

Problem solved. I found a hole in the sofa (courtesy of Miss Daisy Chainsaw in her youth) just large enough to fit my diary in. I will retrieve it whenever I have something to say. And whenever the coast is clear. I'm thinking this will usually be while Miss Daisy is tucking in the oldies at night and I am warming the den up for her return. Genius.

It's been a few days now and nobody has discovered my diary. I am starting to relax a little. And also to muse on the fact that obviously nobody pays that much attention to what I'm doing anyway. Charming.

There are times when you wish you had a tape recorder. This is a word for word account of my conversation with mum this morning. I might need this in court one day.

Mum: "Bailey, did you have an accident by the TV stand?"

Me: "No, I most definitely did not"

Mum: "Was it Daisy?" (yeah, like I'd grass on Miss Daisy – even if it was her)

Me: "Nope. Must have been the old man"

Mum: "Hmmm. Okay, I'll ask him"

Me: "Why bother? We both know he's guilty"

[a moment or two of mutual chuckling]

Mum: "Alright, I won't ask him then"

Me: "That would be best. No point in embarrassing the old codger"

Some thoughts on mum. I call her that because she adopted me. It's a pretty big honour but I doubt she appreciates it. The other one has never done anything for me that I can tell, so I just call him the old man. Or numbnuts. Mum's good for things like cleaning, grooming, providing meals and other girly stuff like that. She's also a terrible nag but then so is Miss Daisy so I guess that's just a female thing. On the whole, I quite like her. She claims it was love at first sight when we first met. For her, I'm sure it was. I mean, why wouldn't it be? For me, it was more like mild interest. I did give her jacket a polite nibbling, though. I think that sealed the deal for her.

Maybe I should write down some of the family history. I'm in the prime of life and plan to stick around for a good while yet, but future generations might wanna hear some of this stuff. If they're clever enough to find my diary, of course, which is unlikely but you never know.

Family Legend No 1: The Relocating

Miss Daisy told me this one as I never knew Whisky. He was her first partner (and soulmate, as she is fond of saying – not very tactful, but whatever). Anyway, a long, long time ago in a house far, far away, the old man built a hutch for Whisky which he lived in for about 3 months. Then he moved into the house. I'm not quite sure how he did this and Miss Daisy is a little hazy on the details too (it was before her time) but I gotta hand it to him, he paved the way for all of us. The fact that the old man did hours and hours of hard labour on the hutch for absolutely no reason is an added bonus and makes Whisky a hero in my opinion. So all hail to Whisky 'The Godfather' – we owe you one, dude. We owe you everything, in fact.

Thought for the day: Is there anybody who actually likes broccoli? Highly unlikely. If it was up to me, I'd exterminate it from the planet. I sense the oldies understand this on some level, hence the fact that it was followed by my favourite pudding, banana. Intriguing – could it be that there is real intelligence there? I have been pondering this question for some time now and have still not reached a solid conclusion.

I think I could be forgiven for feeling a little threatened by Miss Daisy's previous relationship with her 'soulmate', Whisky Chaser. I've seen photos and he was very good looking. I must admit. Tall, dark and handsome. Luckily, I have been blessed with an extremely large ego from birth, which is some compensation for the short legs and tendency towards chubbiness. Thus I was able to woo and win Miss Daisy's paw a mere six months after she lost Whisky. I may not be her soulmate but she loves me. I am her Bunster. As an added bonus, the oldies believe I mended her broken heart, which means they are forever in my debt. I keep quiet about the fact that six months equates to about five years in human terms, so I think Miss Daisy was more than ready for love again. Especially considering she had to live on her own with them for that long. Poor girl – doesn't bear thinking about.

The oldies asked why the biscuit tin was on the floor this morning. I thought quick and told them we have a poltergeist. Was expecting screaming and panic but oddly they didn't react at all. Perhaps they didn't understand poltergeist and I should have said ghost. I always forget to dumb it down for them. Miss Daisy was conspicuously absent when this conversation was going on. She owes me a nose nuzzle. Get in.

Miss Daisy is a total princess. This morning she had me grooming her ears for at least half an hour. How *does* she wrap us all around her paw so easily? I think it's because she was a baby when she moved in and the oldies and Whisky spoiled her rotten. She's never so much as set foot in a cage or hutch and has no idea of how easy she has it. I disapprove, in theory, but still find myself spoiling her also. I really love her, that's the problem. No, I adore her. Worship the ground she hops on, in fact.

The old man. He's a tricky one. On the one hand, I rely on him to rescue me periodically from the annoying girly chatter of mum and Miss Daisy. On the other hand, he releases toxic vapour in my face quite a lot when he's lounging on the sofa. And yet in spite of this constant threat I still often choose to sit at his feet. This is due to the fact that there is a warm spot there, which I have always assumed is something to do with the heating pipes, but now that I think about it perhaps it's caused by the toxic vapour itself? Will need to ponder that one some more.

Miss Daisy is nesting. Suspicious. I'm no expert on these things but (a) she is nearly 7 which is officially elderly, not that she acts like it, and (b) she had her girly operation years ago. Not to mention the fact that (c) I lost my boy balloons right around the time I moved in here. All in all, I think the chances of her producing some babies are pretty slim. Even a stud muffin like me can't work miracles. I'd better tread carefully with this one. Feminine matters are not my forte.

Speaking of boy balloons, it's worth noting that you can take the muffins off the stud but not take the stud out of the stud muffin. Or something like that. The point is, I have *mental* boy balloons and that's what matters. They're also much bigger than the old man's, as proved by my superior skills with the ladies.

The nest building seems to be over, which is a relief, but I hope mum is sensitive enough not to remove the nest from under the bed *just* yet. It took a lot of work, after all, and if Miss Daisy wants to believe there could be some little Bunster/Chainsaw babies there soon, who are we to shatter her dream? I am being even more loving than usual to help her through this crisis.

Miss Daisy told me, and I quote, to stop being so 'clingy' and 'weird'. Then she gave me the ear. At least, I think she did; those lop ears are very pretty and all, but it does make for quite a lot of miscommunication. When I give the ear, it's loud and clear.

Still giving Miss Daisy a wide berth. When she's in a huffle puff, you sure do know about it. She's spent most of the day with the old man. Any port in a storm, I guess. But Miss Daisy is inordinately fond of the old man, by my standards. She usually spends a good part of each day in his 'study' (more like a toxic health hazard filled with crap, if you ask me), sitting at his feet and gazing adoringly at him. Bizarre. It's lucky I'm not the jealous type or that sort of thing could really mess with your head.

Family Legend No 2: The Bonding

When I first heard this story from Miss Daisy I was a little dubious, I must admit. But she assures me it is the truth, so here goes. Back in the day, before Whisky met Daisy, he formed an unusual attachment to the old man – out of desperation, presumably. Poor lad. Apparently he used to follow the old man around, sit under his chair and (urgh) lick his face. Explains a lot. I've often wondered why the old man sometimes looks at me with hopeful eyes. Dream on, numbnuts – I ain't licking no human, not even if you were Brad Pitt himself. Angelina Julie though – yeah, I might lick her. If she begged me.

The oldies say I am rude for not sharing my herbs with Miss Daisy. I say, they don't call me Bailey 'Elbows' Bunster for nothing. When you grow up with five Dutch siblings you learn to fight for your food. Survival of the fattest and all that. I wonder where they all are now? Perhaps we should have a family reunion and compare waistlines. Knowing my luck, I'd probably still be the fattest. But I would definitely have the prettiest girl on my arm.

Had a rather humiliating encounter with the oldies today. Nail trimming time is always excruciating for everyone involved, however, I can make my peace with the actual trimming – it is necessary, after all. But the giggling and comments of 'chunky monkey' and 'oooh, my poor back' were a bit out of order. Of course, Miss Daisy is 'light as a feather' and 'so ladylike'. Discrimination is an ugly thing but my ego has taken quite a battering over the years and still remains intact.

The oldies' insults just roll off me like water off a duck's back.

Miss Daisy and I did some hallway sprinting to test out the new nails. We reckon there is a 10% speed differential. More testing needed, provisionally scheduled for 2am every night this week. We don't want the oldies getting in the way and mucking up our timings. I've collided with their tree trunk legs before at high speed and it's really quite painful.

Didn't move from the den for five solid hours this afternoon. It was awesome. My bladder was bursting a bit by the end, in fact I think a little pee might have slipped out, but tough luck. The snooze was just too good to disturb. The blankets needed washing anyway.

It's really quite annoying when you go into your den and all the blankets are gone. Why does it take *so* long to wash a blanket? Squatting on a piece of bare lino all day is not my idea of a good time. Unacceptable. And when the blankets *were* finally returned, they smelt like Persil. Yuk. Miss Daisy and I spent most of the evening rolling around on them to regain some scent control. It sounds like fun but it really wasn't – it was jolly hard work.

Thought for the day: Is there anything better in life than filling your tummy with herbs and then stretching out for a snooze in the sun? I think not. Especially when your lady spoons you. Pure bliss. Until mum walks in, squeals and grabs her camera, that is. I have a lot of sympathy for celebs – the paparazzi are pure evil.

Interesting philosophical discussion with Miss Daisy today. Subject: The Definition of Love. She argued that love is when you share your food with someone. I disagreed, obviously, on the basis that I love her to bits but still don't like sharing food. I then put forward the argument that love is closeness, based on the fact that when you really love someone you don't mind your whiskers touching. Her eyes went all soft and she tucked her head under my chin and sighed happily, which I took for a clear sign of agreement. So there you have it. The Definition of Love, according to The Bunster, is: Intertwined Whiskers. Maybe I should copyright that.

I think my tail is getting fatter. In fact, I'm sure it is. I can't do a proper visual assessment, obviously, but it just *feels* fatter. I asked Miss Daisy but she just snorted and went back to sleep.

I retrieved the tape measure from the oldies' bedroom (suspicious) in order to measure my tail. Surprisingly difficult. In the end I managed it by holding the end down with one heel and squinting over my shoulder. Official tail measurements are: Length, 4 inches. Girth, 3 ½ inches. Quite proud of that.

Miss Daisy measured my tail *properly* today, as she put it. Revised official tail measurements are: Length, 2 inches. Girth, 1 inch. Disappointing. I cheered myself up by measuring Miss Daisy's dewlap. It took a long, long time and I made sure I measured every little bit of it. Unfortunately, I forgot to write any of the measurements down so I might have to do it all again tomorrow. What a shame.

We have an additional oldie in situ, mum's sister aka 'Auntie B'. I like it when she comes to visit, she gives good strokes – not too hard, not too soft. Plus, she brings cousin Mitch with her. He sleeps in the hallway and guards the front door. Mitch is big, black and gentle – a bit like that bloke from The Green Mile. But with more intelligence and less ability to heal humans.

When I get given a strawberry for no apparent reason, I always get a tad suspicious. It could be straight from Russia and laced with polonium, for all I know. Although it's probably just to make up for the constant chatter from the kitchen – those two never seem to run out of things to say to each other. After a little dubious sniffing, I consented to eat the strawberry. Relieved to report it was polonium free (and delicious).

Auntie B and Mitch have gone home. I spent the day snoozing in front of the TV while the old man watched the British Grand Prix. No disrespect to the girlies but we needed a bit of bloke time. Lewis Hamilton only finished fourth. I feel a bit guilty – I really should have made the trip to Silverstone and helped him out. He's lost without his primary advisor and race mechanic. I did Monaco, obviously. You have to do Monaco.

It is the old man's birthday today and both Miss Daisy and mum told me I had to be nice to him. How annoying - insulting him is usually the highlight of my day. I muttered the insults under my breath instead but it just wasn't the same. I did get a small revenge by hoovering up the cake crumbs from around his toes. I'm pretty sure he was saving them for later. You snooze, you lose, old man.

Did a few laps of the coffee table this morning, followed by some yoga stretches. I try to do this at least once a week. You gotta stay in shape. I encouraged mum to join me (subtle hint) but as usual she declined. Probably easier to just hide the biscuits from her. And she calls *me* fat. The irony, sadly, is completely lost on her.

A mere three days later and now it is Miss Daisy's birthday. What is the oldies' obsession with birthdays? Not that I'm complaining - she was given a new herb variety which I partook of, and then I had a nice lie down in the den while she played with her new toys. No cake, regrettably. So now she is officially 7 years old but she still doesn't look a day over 2, in my opinion. Still beautiful, still a mega hottie. Lucky me – she may be a cradle snatcher but I'm quite happy to be snatched.

More ponderings on the old man. He is invariably polite to me, which is more than I can say for mum and Miss Daisy, and very free with the herbs (when the girls aren't watching). On the other hand, he does spend a ridiculous amount of time 'working'. Time which could be better spent in manly chats and general Bunster worship. His loss, I suppose.

Miss Daisy went on one of her routine trips to the hospital today to get her teeth trimmed. On the upside, I had the den to myself all day and really stretched the old legs out. Awesome. On the downside, she came home reeking of hospital so, as usual, I spent the entire evening grooming her. I'm exhausted. My tongue needs a three week holiday.

Thought for the day: if I ruled the world (and one day I will) the first thing I'd do is introduce the 'Bailey Bunster Universal Law of Snuggling' and make all humans snuggle for at least an hour a day. Should stop all wars

---

dead in their tracks, I reckon. There's nothing like a good snuggle for making you forget all your problems.

One of the old man's friends has come to stay. There is less room on the sofa now but on the whole I approve. He fulfils the most basic roommate requirements, namely (a) he watches where he steps, (b) he gives a decent nose rub, and (c) he keeps his mumblings below 10 decibels. He's also not quite as smelly as the old man. I shall allow him to stay.

Composed a telegram to the oldies, as follows. "HERB SITUATION CRITICAL STOP DOWN TO LAST RATION STOP GET OFF BUM AND GO TO SHOP STOP FROM BB STOP PS DO NOT IGNORE ME STOP". Now to find somewhere that still sends telegrams. I really should get an email account.

Let that be a lesson to me. I was just getting mildly fond of the new oldie and now he's gone. Never invest in an unknown human.

Seems my telegram made it through after all. Excellent herb ration today. Miss Daisy made a swift exit. Herbs make me honky. I can't help it – the tail goes up and the honk is on. Bunster to the max.

Family Legend No 3: The Honking

I don't actually remember much from when I moved in here. I had only recently lost my boy balloons and was still in a hormonal haze. And it *was* 2 years ago now. But there was a lot of honking. And a lot of chasing. Luckily for Miss Daisy, slightly chubby, vertically challenged rabbits can't jump so she was able to escape me pretty easily. I remember her looking down at me from the sofa, bed or whatever and laughing her head off while I chased my tail in circles, looking for her. And I remember the honking. So much honking. I also vaguely remember a stuffed sheep that I got quite fond of. Good times.

Today I put together a simple herb ratings system, as follows:-

Bailey Bunster's Honky Herbs Ratings:-

Woodlands (all varieties): enjoyable but no honk

Burgess Mountain Meadow: partial honking

Burgess Country Garden: mega honk honk honk

Tests are on-going and new herbage always welcome. In fact, I wonder if Burgess need an in-house herb tester? My schedule is always busy but I'm sure I can make space in it somewhere for *that* job. Really must get that email account sorted and drop them a line. I'm sure they'd leap at the chance to work with The Bunster. Who wouldn't?

Another confrontation with mum about the mysterious pee puddle that appears now and then. She says she knows it's me because she 'recognises my pee'. She seriously needs to get a life. And some solid proof. This could easily be classed as slander. I may really have to take legal advice if this continues.

Miss Daisy and I spent the day devising a cunning plan to move dinner time forward by one hour. It's more cunning than Baldrick himself. Key weapons to be deployed are: (1) Harassment, (2) Intimidation, (3) Pleading Eyes. Bit worried about the last one – not sure I can pull it off convincingly. I'll focus on the first two.

The oldies are so easily entertained, bless them. Simple minds, simple pleasures. I think Deadliest Catch was made especially for them. And Ice Road Truckers. If I cared enough, I'd be embarrassed for them. Instead, I usually feign polite interest by pointing one ear at the TV and simply let my mind drift to pondering higher matters. Things like, what is the biggest banana in the world? And why has it not been delivered to me yet? Puzzling.

Thought for the day: If we weren't here, would the oldies ever leave the sofa? Doubtful. Miss Daisy says if there was a human herding contest she'd win because she can herd mum off the sofa and into the kitchen in less than a minute. It's true, she can - it's amazing to watch. The old man is a bit more of a challenge – we don't call him 'Velcro Butt' for nothing.

Had a full speed, head-on collision with mum's anklebone this morning and she had the nerve to say 'ouch'! What about my poor nose? Maybe I should double up and sue her for that as well as the allegations of pee puddles that I know absolutely nothing about. I had to rest my sore nose in a bowl of medicinal herbs for an hour or so. I just about managed to eat some of them.

Update on the dinner time campaign. Time gained so far: 22 minutes. We're nearly half way there and well ahead of our 2 week schedule. The begging mat by the kitchen door is seeing a lot of action and Miss Daisy has the pleading eyes thing off pat. I'm doing a lot of shoulder squaring and threatening ear pointing to back her up. I love it when a plan comes together.

For every action there is a reaction. And for every insult there is a revenge. I will cite as an example a conversation with mum today:

Mum: "Get your *fat, greedy* nose out of there Bailey"

Me: "Oh, I thought you'd put the herbs in already..."

Mum: "I haven't put the herbs in yet"

Me: "Well, I can't move my nose *now*. I might miss some herbs"

Mum: "But I can't put the herbs in with your nose in the way..."

Me: (patiently) "I already told you, I can't move my nose"

Mum: (through clenched teeth) "But I can't... unless you move..."

This could have continued on for hours if Miss Daisy hadn't come along and broken it up. She is way too soft on the oldies.

Mission accomplished on the dinner time campaign. On time and within budget. Revised dinner time is now officially 8pm. Was it worth it? Probably not but you have to keep the old brain cells ticking over. No doubt the oldies will backslide anyway and we'll have to do it all again.

Spent most of the afternoon detoxifying myself after a misguided foray into the old man's study. How on earth does Miss Daisy stand it? Maybe if you grow up with the smell from a baby, you get some kind of immunity to it. Maybe (horrible thought) she actually *likes* it.

I'm rather glad that I haven't known the oldies since I was a baby. It means I can get away with telling them all sorts of implausible stories about what I've done in my life. For example, this evening they were wittering on about the war in Afghanistan in an unbearable 'know it all' fashion. I nodded along sagely for a while and then said "Of course, it was all different when I was there. We had to dig our fox holes with our bare paws while the Teletubbies were attacking us from all sides. The new guys don't know how easy they have it". Then I looked away into the middle distance with a pained expression on my face, as if reliving hard memories. After a moment of stunned (and presumably respectful) silence, they changed the subject. Bunster wins again.

Not good news on the oldie front. Mum says she is going away for a week. I most definitely did not authorise that. If this affects my schedule, I will not be a happy Bunster.

Mum left this morning for her trip and the schedule is slipping already. Dinner was served at 8.42pm i.e. 42 minutes *late*. Or is it possible that the old man is oblivious to the fact that we recently changed our dinner time to 8pm? He *does* have his head up his backside most of the time so this is quite likely. He probably thought he was doing us a favour with an early dinner. Idiot.

Dinner was served at 9pm precisely. Looks like we are back on the old routine. He's a cunning old fox at times. It goes against everything I believe in to say it but... kudos to the old man.

Three days in and the place is starting to smell even worse than usual. The health hazard that is the old man's study seems to be spreading like a toxic virus. Even Miss Daisy has started tutting at him about the dirty crockery littering every surface, the piles of laundry mounting up etc, etc. She is still oddly immune to the smell though and stuck to him like glue.

Only two more days to go, says Miss Daisy, wistfully. She's really loving it, having the old man to herself. I barely see either of them from sunrise to sunset. At least I've got the den to myself but it's very quiet without mum click-clacking away on her keyboard all day long. I almost miss her.

Whispered conversation between Miss Daisy and the old man this evening (while he was sprawled on the sofa and she was balancing on his chest):

Old man: "Shall we give Bailey a raisin too?"

Miss Daisy: (giggling) "No, he's too fat anyway"

Old man: (disapproving) "Oh Dazo, he's not"

Miss Daisy: "He is so! Give it to me, daddy"

Old man: "Oh alright then. Naughty pickle"

Did they think I couldn't hear them? Or do they just not care? Outrageous. The fact that shortly thereafter I was given several raisins does not make up for it at all. Went to bed in a grump.

Manic clean-up by the old man, heroically assisted by Miss Daisy. Presumably this heralds mum's imminent return. About time too – I'm getting fed up with wading through rubbish and holding my paw over my nose.

[later] She's back. I greeted her with a casual "wotcha?" and retreated to the den. Can't give her the impression I missed her at all, her ego would be uncontrollable.

Happy Bunster.

AUTUMN

Went to the docs for a physical today. Disappointing weigh-in results - I have gained *nothing*. Still 2.4kg and the doc can still feel my ribs. Doc said I'm at my ideal weight, which obviously won't do. Need to bulk up on bananas, I think.

Oldies are acting all lovey-dovey around each other. Quite sickening. Apparently it is a 'special day' for them. I wish they'd take their 'specialness' elsewhere. Siberia, preferably.

After yesterday's disgraceful PDAs, I've been doing some pondering on the oldies' relationship. They seem pretty happy. I think this is mostly thanks to me, Miss Daisy and Whisky, though. You can't live with blissfully loved up couples like us for years and not have *some* of their good influence rub off on you. Yet another thing they should be thanking us for, but rarely do.

Thought for the day: 'I eat, therefore I am'. Old Socrates nearly got it right, bless him. Disappointingly, the oldies tell me there is an international shortage of bananas and I must gain weight the hard way, by eating hay. I retaliated with a request for a double herb ration. After a little haggling, we struck a deal. Herb ration has been increased by precisely one-fifth. I can work with that. Will need to cut down on unnecessary exercise though. From now on it's strictly loo visits only. The rest is den time.

It occurred to me that the oldies are really nothing more than glorified food dispensers. You nudge the leg a bit and hey presto, food descends from above like magic. And if it breaks, you just have to give it a bit of welly to get it going again. 'Welly' in Miss Daisy's book is a good ankle nipping. In my book, it's an icy, penetrating gaze delivered from under threateningly lowered ears. Never fails.

Another trip to the docs. Doc said I am now on the verge of being 'fat' and have put on 80 grams. He told mum (cos she's a bit thick) that that's the same weight as Mars bar. Never occurred to either of them that I might have just eaten a Mars bar. He's as thick as mum.

Later on at home mum said, with some admiration, how is it possible to put on 80g in a week? I said, when your name is Bailey Bunster, *anything* is possible, especially when food is involved. Challenge met and

exceeded, I'd say.   I'm pretty sure I can kiss goodbye
to the increased herb ration though.

Miss Daisy spent half an hour making herself the perfect
nest in the blankets, and then I stole it. I'm so bad, but
it feels *so* good. It was a bit of a tight fit, mind. Had to
do a good bit of wiggling to enlarge it sufficiently to get
my backside in.

Have been wondering why Whisky got a cool nickname
like 'Torro', Miss Daisy gets called 'Chainsaw' or 'Dazo'
and I get stuck with things like 'Chubster', 'Fatty' and,
worst of all, 'Boo Boo'? Thankfully the last one is only
from mum and usually accompanied by a good back
scratching, which makes it slightly more forgivable. Plus
I get a small revenge by calling her 'Moo Moo' behind
her back.   Still, I think this counts as blatant
discrimination and if I were ever to leave I could
probably do them for constructive dismissal.   I'll add
that to the list for my lawyer.

2am.   Just got kicked out of the bedroom in a very
undignified fashion.   Miss Daisy is currently camping
outside the bedroom door in protest and giving it a

---

good digging at regular intervals. I have retreated to the den in high dudgeon. I don't appreciate being moved by a *foot*, however gently. Bordering on Bunster abuse, I'd say.

Thought for the day, courtesy of the late, great JFK: 'Ask not what your Bunster can do for you... ask what you can do for your Bunster'. Might print this on a label and put it on the fridge door. The oldies expect far too much from me without giving anything in return. They need a wakeup call.

Three days later and our bedroom privileges have still not been reinstated. They could really be serious this time. It's a bit of a cheek considering they usually keep *us* awake with their snoring. I don't really care anyway – Miss Daisy and I have been having some awesome den snuggles. She's such a fidget bum when the oldies are in the vicinity. It's nice to get some proper rest.

Broccoli for dinner. I thought I'd made my feelings on this perfectly clear but apparently not. Miss Daisy gamely ate most of it while I retreated to the den in a grump. She's far too polite.

Broccoli *again*. They're taking the mickey now. Or –
scary thought – they have outsmarted me for once. I
am losing weight at a dangerous rate.

There's a bit of a nip in the air now. Makes me feel
young and sprightly. I tried a bit of the old 'honk and
chase' with Miss Daisy but it was not appreciated.
Apparently there is a fine line between 'flattering
attention' and 'harassment' and I have crossed that line.
I told her it's actually a disability to be born a red-
blooded stud muffin and she should be a bit more
understanding. She just sniffed and jumped on the
sofa. I'm sure I heard her mutter something how she
misses living with a 'real' gentleman. Whisky,
presumably. How rude.

Family Legend No 4: The Jumping

I've never actually heard this one before, Miss Daisy just
told it to me this evening. Apparently when Whisky was
quite elderly he had an operation and the oldies thought
they should keep Miss Daisy away from him afterwards
so she wouldn't mess with his stitches (shows how
much *they* know, idiots). So anyway, they set up a

barrier in the door and put her in the hallway. She said, with a certain amount of smugness, that the barrier was waist high on the old man and she cleared it in one. She jumped straight over it like it wasn't there. Considering I find it a struggle to make it onto the sofa, I am very impressed. And told her so.

Better get started on my winter coat. I really, really hate moulting. Makes me grumpy, makes Miss Daisy grumpy, makes the oldies grumpy. Makes the vacuum cleaner grumpy, for that matter. Plus, I run the constant risk of having a tuft whipped out by a passing oldie. They have *no* idea how much that smarts. Or they do know and still do it anyway, which is even worse.

Had a minor brainwave and googled 'black high waisted pants with a balloon seat, size XXL'. But seems nobody makes them. Maybe I should give Simon Cowell a ring and ask him where he gets his from. The only problem with that solution is that I'd have to speak to Simon Cowell. Oh well, guess I will have to do the winter coat the old fashioned way. Moult mode officially engaged.

The old man's friend is back and it is *his* birthday, apparently. Just another excuse for cake, if you ask me. Greedy guts oldies. I took pity on him and allowed him to stroke me for one minute. He was quite rightly very grateful; without that, his birthday would have sucked.

Regretting that stroke now. Honestly, you do someone a favour and they repay you by comparing you to a Space Hopper. This is a step too far. Granted, my ears do bear a certain resemblance to a Space Hopper's ears (although I prefer to think of them as McLaren Racing ears). Granted, my backside is unusually round. But I am not orange. So either he is colour blind or stupid. Probably both. The only consolation I can take from this is that he is old enough to remember Space Hoppers.

Mr 'Space Hopper' has gone and never to return, it is to be hoped. The oldies seem to enjoy having him around but I wouldn't trust their judgement anyway. Losers, the lot of them. Space Hopper, indeed. Ridiculous. I do wish Miss Daisy would stop giggling about it.

Another 'spa day' for Miss Daisy, aka teeth trimming. Visited the study to spend some time with the old man. It wasn't that bad actually. Once you learn to breathe through your mouth, the smell becomes almost tolerable. Conversation went something like this:

Me: "You smell"

Old man: "Thanks Bunster"

Me: "Have you considered bathing?"

Old man: "I had a shower this morning"

Me: "You wouldn't know it. Might I suggest a pressure wash system?"

Old man: "OK, I'll think about that"

Me: "And some sort of industrial soap"

Old man: "Yup, OK, that too"

Me: "Just trying to help"

Old man: "Thank you Bailey, I appreciate it"

Me: "You're welcome. You really need to stop smelling"

Old man: "Yeah I got that. Can I do some work now?"

Me: "If you must. Later, potater"

He is very lucky to have me here to give such wise advice. I think he knows that.

The moult is going quite well, so far. Tidemark is currently residing just above the buttocks.

The oldies are being very rude about my moult line. I do *not* look like I'm wearing Superman pants. And if I was Superman, I'd sure as hay not stick around here to be insulted. I'd take my Lois Lane (Miss Daisy) and fly off to find a banana plantation. I would *not* invite the oldies to visit. Ever.

Thought for the day, courtesy of The Cat from Red Dwarf: 'If I don't nap 9 or 10 times a day, I don't have enough energy for my main snooze'. That's very true, that is. I must admit, I never thought I'd be agreeing with a cat but you have to give credit where it's due.

Our bedroom privileges have been reinstated (weekends only) and we are most definitely *not* abusing it. We were quiet as mice this morning, just a little magazine nibbling here and there. Nothing that would wake mum up, that's for sure, but the old man has ears on elastic. Still, we only got kicked out at 6am so that's an improvement.

Was lying on the rug this evening, minding my own business and watching TV, when the old man lifted his leg and let out the most vile smelling fart I have *ever* encountered. And I've encountered a good many. If I could vomit, I would have. May have to invest in a gas mask.

Still recovering from yesterday's gas attack. That stuff sure does linger in your fur. I think if the UN got hold of a sample, they'd probably classify it as a biological weapon. I'll try and get him to fart in a jar next time so I can send them a sample. Gotta do my civic duty.

It is very puzzling that the oldies purchased a new mattress which is too high for us to jump onto. Not that I ever go up there, I prefer to keep all four feet firmly on the ground whenever possible. But Miss Daisy does enjoy bouncing off their tummies in the morning, clambering over their heads and putting her paws in their eye sockets. I don't want her to be deprived. I'm assuming some sort of staircase will be installed in due course.

It is even more puzzling that the oldies will spend hundreds of pounds on a mattress for themselves, but not fork out twenty quid for a staircase. Instead, we get a cardboard box filled with scrap paper. The upside of this is that it's excellent gnawing material. They really are gluttons for punishment.

Yet another birthday – mum's, this time. I helped the old man make her a carrot cake (by supervising from a distance) and resisted the temptation to nibble her flowers. Being 'good' is really quite exhausting. And boring. Miss Daisy on the other hand had a whale of a time helping mum rip her presents open. By the time she'd finished, the living room was covered in wrapping paper confetti. Quite brightened the place up, actually.

Took delivery of a Super Kingsize Hungarian Goosedown Duvet today. It's very kind of the oldies but I'm not sure I'll fit it in the den. I'll give it a jolly good try though.

[later] the duvet's for *them*, apparently. What a waste.

Miss Daisy really is a clever little minx. She gives my ears a few licks while she's doing her dewlap and in return I get the 'honour' of grooming her from head to toe. I have been giving her the good Bunster lovin' all day - ears, eyes, nose, the lot - and she *still* wants more. Women. They're never happy.

Embarrassing head on collision with Miss Daisy this morning during the breakfast feet circling. I definitely heard a giggle from above and a rude remark about coconuts knocking together but I chose to let this one go – you have to pick your battles.

It is an awesome feeling when the oldies find your Groom Spot, or 'G Spot' as I like to call it. Never mind the fact that it took them over six months to find it, the important thing is that they now know exactly what I like. Just above the tail, in a scratching movement. Gets me licking the floor in ecstasy, it's so good. Miss Daisy claims she doesn't have a G Spot but I have my suspicions – I've seen her half close her eyes when she's getting an ear rubbing from the old man. She can fool him but she can't fool the Bunster.

A new legend is born, courtesy of Miss Daisy. Very proud of her right now.

Family Legend No 5: The Peeinq

This evening the old man picked up Miss Daisy to give her some medicine. Either this surprised her or she was on her way to the loo, because next minute the old man was standing there with a shocked look on his face while pee cascaded all over him. I laughed so much I nearly wet myself too.

At times like this I love Miss Daisy so much I feel my heart will burst.

I believe the 'midnight' carrot should be renamed 'the-sometime-before-we-drag-our-butts-to-bed' carrot. The oldies get lazier every day. According to Miss Daisy, the midnight carrot is a long tradition stretching back to Whisky's time and it has very rarely, if ever, been delivered at midnight. The irony of this has yet to register with the oldies, which is unsurprising considering their general intelligence. I'm not sure they even know what irony *is,* to be honest.

This evening I have been thoroughly abused and taken advantage of. The source of this abuse is, of course, mum:

Mum: "Do you want a bum scratch, Bailey?"

Me: "Don't mind if I do, thank you"

Mum: "How's that?"

Me: "Perfect, keep going"

Mum: "Let me just get those tufts out for you..."

Me: "No, they're fine... leave them"

Mum: "C'mon, just a little bit... "

Me: "I said leave them, woman!"

Whereupon she completely ignored my direct order and whipped the tufts out. Never mind the fact that it hurts worse than waxing, it's theft – plain and simple. She's lucky I didn't phone the police. Retreated to the den in a mega grump.

Still grumping in the den. The problem is, this leaves my mind free to wander. Like today, it occurred to me that I haven't had banana for so long, I've forgotten what it tastes like. Surely the international shortage has been resolved by now? I think the oldies are holding out on me.

Emerged from my grump today only to find out that the herb supply is running dangerously low and my dealer (pet shop down the road) is away on holiday for a week. Sometimes I just wanna punch the oldies in the face they're so stupid. Back to den grumping.

Well, it seems someone does hear our prayers after all. I was presented with a banana today and, once I'd managed to stop drooling, grabbed a good few mouthfuls. Old 'Hamster Cheeks' Bunster strikes again. I have announced an official end to the grump. Miss Daisy and mum breathed a big sigh of relief in unison.

Miss Daisy really is getting soft in her old age. This evening mum fell asleep on the sofa (mouth open, legs open - *not* an attractive sight, thank goodness she was wearing trousers) and Miss Daisy laid down against her foot and fell asleep too. What was she thinking? I suppose if you live with them for that long you must get quite fond of them, although I can't really imagine it yet. I'm still at the tolerance stage. Anyway, the old man managed to get a picture of them which could come in handy one day for blackmail and so on. We also heroically resisted the urge to fetch some crayons, bowls of water etc and mess with them while they were sleeping.

---

10 laps of the coffee table today. That's a personal best. Maybe I should try out for the Olympics after all. Bailey Bolt. I'm sure I can give that Jamaican a run for his money.

Mum is displaying classic symptoms of an imminent cleaning frenzy, including increased irritation and narky comments about fur and 'nuts'. Miss Daisy and I are preparing the den for a siege and laying in good supplies of herbs and hay. We're gonna call it 'The Love In'. I suggested a banner a la John and Yoko, but Miss Daisy said that would be a bit OTT. She suggested flowers but I said that would be a bit girly. Oh well, we don't need props to prove our love anyway.

Speaking of 'nuts', that reminds me of another family legend.

Family Legend No 6: The Sniffing

Miss Daisy told me this one – in between giggles. Not that she was even there, she heard it from Whisky. Apparently one day when mum was much younger and even more stupid, she picked up a handful of Whisky's 'nuts' aka poo and sniffed it. That's right, she sniffed it. Why? I don't think even *she* knows that. I'm sure it smelled delightful anyway. She's welcome to smell *my* nuts any day.

Day 2 of 'The Love In'. I'm gaining a new appreciation of the den. I take it for granted most of the time but it's really pretty awesome. It's amazing to think it's been occupied by Whisky too in the past. I'm literally treading in the footprints of the great. I am quite in awe of Whisky Chaser. From what Miss Daisy tells me, he carried out the initial training of the oldies with great patience and dignity. Considering that this was years ago now and their current stupidity *still* makes me want to bash their heads together on a regular basis, I really don't know how he did it. Patience of a saint, if you ask me.

Day 3 of 'The Love In'. Why *are* the oldies so obsessed with cleanliness? In my humble opinion, they should be spending a lot more time on their personal hygiene which, quite frankly, leaves a lot to be desired. Most of the time they only bathe once a day. Disgusting. I have at least 10 baths a day, minimum. And I give Miss Daisy about 5 baths a day. You'd think they'd take the hint.

I smell like Dettox and have a Dyson-like buzzing in my ears but the spring clean is over. 'The Love In' is also over, regrettably. Never mind, the den needs a clean anyway. Better get mum onto that right away.

Conversation with mum this morning:

Mum: "Bailey, are you kidding me?"

Me: (wide eyed innocence) "Sorry, what?"

Mum: (pointing at the puddle by the TV stand) "That!!"

Me: (inspecting puddle) "Ahhh... yes, I *thought* I heard the old man sleepwalking last night... maybe he should see a doctor, it looks a bit red"

Mum: (walks off) "Whatever, Bails"

She has absolutely *no* sense of humour when she's been cleaning. How boring.

It's Bonfire Night, which means it's November, which means it's definitely winter. And the heating is *still* not on in the morning. The oldies say there is a recession on and we can't have the heating on 24-7. Well, that ain't my problem. I need to check the paperwork but I do believe that the adoption papers which mum signed state that a constant temperature of between 12 and 20 degrees Celsius must be maintained year round. It's so cold I have to break the layer of ice on my water bowl in the mornings. OK, that's a slight exaggeration but either way it's jolly cold. I'd be alright if I had a Hungarian Goosedown Duvet, I'm sure. Alright for some.

Thought for the day: 'In sub-zero temperatures, it is necessary to eat twice as much as usual'. This is a well-known fact oft quoted by arctic explorers but I think I can safely say it applies to me too at the moment. I am at severe risk of hypothermia. Have a new sympathy for Captain Scott sitting in his hut, scribbling in his diary and writing letters to his loved ones at home. Poor chap. If I freeze to death maybe *my* diary will be discovered and put in a museum one day. That would be pretty cool. Not the freezing to death bit, the museum bit.

I was poised to dial the RSPCA Helpline today when Miss Daisy intervened and said to 'leave it to her'. No harm in letting her have a try, I suppose. I should still report mum though – she's clearly been ignoring all the clauses about banana and herbage supplies also. Really must dig out that paperwork.

Conversation overheard this morning while loitering outside the study door:

Miss Daisy: "Brrrrrrrr"

Old man: "What's up poppet? Are you chilly?"

Miss Daisy: "Mmmm... little bit"

Old man: "Poor Dazo... I'll fix that for you"

Two seconds later he emerged at high speed, nearly flattening me against the wall, and literally raced down the hallway to put the heating on. Miss Daisy's power over him never fails to amaze me. If I had asked, I would have got told something like "Don't be daft, you've got plenty of flab to keep you warm, Bunster. Do some exercise if you're feeling cold". Double standards or what.

Now that I come to think of it, Miss Daisy is looking a little bit fragile. Her beautiful dewlap is as full and radiant as ever but I can feel her ribs when I'm grooming her and that doesn't seem right at all. She's still eating as much as me. Puzzling.

Mum told me off for 'barging' Miss Daisy off the food bowl. I apologised but pointed out that in my defence I can't help being Dutch and therefore obsessed with food. She said, somewhat huffily, that I was talking rubbish and that obsession is a strong word. Then she said (cattily) that perhaps I should see a shrink about my 'obsession'. So I said thanks for the offer, stretched out on the rug, closed my eyes and started talking. When I opened them half an hour later, she'd left the room. So much for wanting to help me with my issues.

Miss Daisy went to the doctor *again*. And her teeth are just fine. I sense a disturbance in the force. Worried Bunster.

The oldies have been making a big fuss of Miss Daisy and (outrage) sneaking her extra food on the sly.

Luckily, I have ears on radar and am able to detect the rustle of nuggets from fifty paces. I usually get there in time to help her lick the bowl out.

Auntie B arrived this evening to stay for the weekend. Miss Daisy spent the entire day preparing - running around making up Mitch's bed, filling up his water bowl and grooming herself every 10 minutes. If she was trying to make me jealous, it worked. Mitch and Miss Daisy spent some time gazing lovingly at each other over the threshold of the hallway door. I couldn't hear what they were saying but I'm guessing they were comparing notes on aches and pains. Mitch is pretty elderly too. The chat from the kitchen sounded more sombre than usual.

Auntie B and Mitch have just left. Miss Daisy seems a little depressed and has gone off to see the old man in his study. Although I know for a fact she is being given extra food in there, I've decided to respect her privacy. My own fat reserves are well stocked at the moment anyway.

I spent hours today bulldozing the blankets and creating a little nest for Miss Daisy. Then I pulled a corner of the blanket over her and wedged her in nice and tight. Mum looked down from her desk and went all gooey eyed. Pathetic. Still, a few extra brownie points never hurt anyone. Looking forward to an increased herb ration tomorrow.

Another trip to the doctor for Miss Daisy. He gave her some medicine which she takes on a little bit of Weetabix. She said it tastes alright and makes her feel better. Feeling quite kindly towards the old doc for once. I always thought he was good for nothing but little pricks and backside inspections.

Miss Daisy doesn't want to play much these days. That's ok with me, I've never been a big player. Not in *that* sense, anyway. We are spending a lot of time snuggling in the den. She told me today that she thinks she'll be leaving soon. She's quite happy about it, says she can't wait to see Whisky again. I must have looked a little forlorn because she then gave me a kiss and told me I'd be ok. She also gave me a small lecture about taking care of the oldies. She's more worried about leaving them than me, which is understandable. They'd be lost without us.

I think I'm gonna stash you for a little while, diary. No offence but I've got a feeling this is not going to be a part of my life I want to remember in great detail. And I want to spend every minute I can with Miss Daisy. Every minute she'll allow me, that is. Her body may be getting weaker but her spirit sure isn't. Still feisty, still running rings around me. What will I do without her?

Gloomy Bunster.

WINTER

Hello diary. So, I'm back. And I regret to report that I am now alone. Miss Daisy has gone to the other place. It's ok though, she was getting very tired and she wanted to go. She is reunited with Whisky and no doubt having a lovely time regaling him with stories of me and the oldies. As for me, I'm having not such a lovely time. The oldies have been in a pretty bad way. Mum keeps disappearing into the kitchen and reappearing with red eyes. As for the old man, he's barely come out of his study for days. Might have to take some action on this, they are being very silly. It's not like we're never gonna see her again. Well, I definitely will anyway. To be honest, I'm not sure whether they'd let the oldies in but probably best not to mention that just at the moment.

I suspect the old man is gaining some comfort from having me sleep under his side of the bed every night. Normally this would be reason enough in itself to stop doing it, but I've decided to take pity on the old boy and will continue to help him out. For a while, anyway. Can't let him think I've gone soft.

Watched mum make an absolute pig's ear of writing our Christmas cards; she seems to have lost the ability to write. She's going through an awful lot of tissues too. I really should have anticipated this and told my stockbroker to buy some shares in Kleenex. I'd be a millionaire by now. I'm sure the old man has got several boxes on the go in his study as well.

Feeling rather smothered. I am The Bunster, not some mummy's boy, I don't need checking on every five minutes and I definitely don't need kisses (urgh). I could do with some more herbs though. You're never really alone if you have a full dish of herbs.

Conversation with mum today:

Mum: "I miss her so much, Bunster"

Me: "I know. Me too. It's ok"

Mum: (crying) "But why is she not here?"

Me: (patiently) "Cos she's gone to the other place"

Mum: "But it's not fair…"

Me: "Don't be silly. You've still got me, haven't you? *And* the old man, for what it's worth… not much, I'm sure, but it's something… pull yourself together, woman"

Mum: (sniffing) "You're quite right Bails. Love you"

Me: "Yeah, don't you forget it"

Honestly, what would she do without me? I dread to think. Getting quite fed up with the damp furs though. Does she not have any stuffed toys she could cry on? Or the old man's shoulder, if she's really desperate.

Mum's oldies are here for dinner. I call them the 'super oldies' although there's really nothing super about them. They invariably either trip over me or put their feet in my way so I trip over *them*. Lots of tripping, anyway. And not the good kind. I'm quite fond of the old beans though. And mum has a faint smile on her face for the first time in ages.

To misquote the Queen, I have a feeling this will be my 'monthus horribilus'. My left eye has been feeling decidedly odd for a while and even the oldies noticed today that it is somewhat bulgy. I told mum it's probably glaucoma. She googled it, looked down at me and said "It's probably glaucoma, Bails". Duh.

Had the bulgy eye checked by the doc. He agreed that it is larger than the other and sent me home. What a pointless waste of time. *And* I had to endure mum's driving for no good reason. Conversations in the car always go something like this:

Me: "That's a red light ahead"

Mum: "Yes, I see it Bunster"

Me: "Well, don't you think you should start slowing down?"

Mum: "It's miles away yet"

Me: "If I bang my nose, I won't be happy"

Mum: "You're never happy"

Me: "That's not true... I'm happy when I'm *not in the car with YOU*"

Frosty silence the rest of the way home.

Went back to the doc for a proper pressure check. As I thought, it is glaucoma. Hereditary, one presumes, as I am nowhere near old enough to get glaucoma. The oldies are to 'keep an eye on it'. Ba boom. I'm glad someone thinks my ailment is amusing, although I do admit it doesn't affect me much. It's more the embarrassment of having glaucoma. I'm almost glad Miss Daisy is not here to laugh at me too. Almost.

A large green tree has taken up residence in our living room. This happens every year. I wonder if it's the same tree? I think it probably is as Miss Daisy always welcomed it like a long lost friend. She loved that tree. I wish she could have seen it one more time. I will give the trunk a little nibble in her honour.

Family Legend No 7: The Nicknaming

The story of how Miss Daisy got her 'Chainsaw' nickname goes right back to her first Christmas, when she wasn't even 1 year old. The green tree was once again in residence and Miss Daisy apparently trimmed it very neatly all the way round the bottom, just above head height. Good for her – leaves more room for presents. It's funny how it always grows back every year though.

I do wish the oldies wouldn't cover the poor tree in all that glittery rubbish. Makes it look quite tawdry. And as for the poor fairy on the top with a branch up her skirt, makes me wince every time I look at it. Still no presents under it. Could it be that they don't trust me not to open them before Christmas? Surely not.

The second set of 'super oldies' has arrived for a visit. These ones belong to the old man. Judging by the amount of crap they brought with them, they'll be staying for a while. Tempted to board up the den and get the oldies to pass my food in on a tray. I'd soundproof it if I could.

The super oldies sure can talk. I'm hoping I'll be given some ear plugs for Christmas. On the plus side, they do make my oldies get their butts off the sofa and outdoors, where the normal people are. Just what they need at the moment. They're doing my head in, hanging around here all day long, moping.

Christmas Day, at last. I thought it would never come. Auntie B has arrived for lunch which, knowing mum's cooking skills, will probably be served at about 5pm. And finally there's a whole heap of presents shoved under the (untrimmed) tree. I'm assuming most of them are for me. Feeling quite perky for the first time in ages.

[later] Happy to report that I did get a good few presents. Herb supplies are looking good and I am no longer worried about running out if we get snowed in. The oldies always assure me this won't happen but I say you never know and better safe than sorry. I prefer to have at least two bags in reserve at all times. Anyway, my best present by far was 'Long Bailey'. Auntie B made him to lie by the door and keep the drafts out. He looks just like me (not quite as handsome, obviously) except that he is long and thin whereas I am round and fat. He's even got my white nozzle. I think we're gonna be good pals. He'll be a better conversationalist than the oldies, that's for sure.

Super oldies have just informed me they are leaving tomorrow. There goes my Christmas perkiness. Was just getting quite used to having them around. Why does nothing last? Feeling gloomy. Back to the den. It still smells faintly of Miss Daisy. Quite comforting. Although perhaps mum should get her act together and wash the blankets now.

The oldies must be fonder of me than previously realised. They are clearly sparing no expense with the old bulgy eye. Today we visited the equivalent of Harley Street, complete with hushed waiting room and pretty nurses. The doc himself had soothing, gentle hands and an excellent bedside manner despite bearing an uncanny resemblance to Hannibal Lecter. I cracked a joke about Chianti but he just looked puzzled. I guess he hasn't seen the film.

It's no fun being a single bun. Trying to get a decent conversation out of the oldies is like trying to get carrot juice out of a lemon. Have been talking a lot to Long Bailey. He's a good listener.

It's been a while now since Miss Daisy left and as the oldies clearly aren't gonna do anything about my single status, I have drafted an advert for the local paper, as follows:

"Middle-aged, slightly chubby but devilishly handsome Dutchie WLTM young, gorgeous, fluffy, uncritical and adoring female with GSOH for snuggles in the den, fine herby dining, hallway cruising and honking. Pls send RECENT photo to PO Box 'BB'"

After some moral deliberation, have decided against the advert. Royal Mail struggles enough as it is – trying to deliver all the responses would completely overwhelm them. Guess I will just have to wait for the oldies to sort themselves out. Lucky I have you to keep me company, diary.

My New Year's resolutions (so far):

1. Eat more
2. Exercise less
3. Be stricter with the oldies
4. Pee on the TV stand more often
5. Buy a banana farm

Already well on my way with the first two and 3 and 4 should be a doddle. The last one might have to wait until I've gotten hold of one of the oldies' credit cards.

Have updated the list:

6. Google yourself regularly
7. Get the final toggle off mum's slippers

That toggle has eluded me for months, if not years. This year, it will be mine. Oh yes it will.

Back to Harley Street. The eye doc spent half an hour shining bright lights in my eye and poking it with things, which I bore with my usual dignity and good humour, then gave me some new eye drops to try for two weeks. Judging by how pale mum went when she saw the bill, they must be top notch.

Having quite a lot of fun with the oldies trying to get eye drops into me twice a day. And on a strict time schedule too. They've tried bribery, cajoling, veiled threats of dinner denial and brute force. It takes them about half an hour on average to corner me and pin me down... and at least three hours afterwards to make it up to me. And the really beautiful thing about it? The eye drops themselves don't bother me at all. Sometimes life just hands you a gift.

Conversation with mum this morning:

Mum: "Are you lonely, Bunster?"

Me: "Well, duh. I thought you'd never ask... also, I'm feeling a bit peckish..."

Mum: (rudely ignoring my hint for herbs) "Shall we get you a friend?"

Me: "Well, if you really insist... but make sure she's a hottie, please"

Needless to say, the thought of only the oldies for company for the rest of my life is truly horrifying and I am more than ready for a little female company. Can't wait, in fact. Now to see whether mum can identify a 'hottie' according to B. Bunster. Doubtful, I'd say.

Mum went off to the adoption centre today and returned with a knowing smile on her face. I asked for a polaroid but she just looked hurt and said "Don't you trust me, Bails?". Course I don't. Quite worried now.

I might have to start putting a bit more faith in mum. The new girl is here and she is a hottie for sure. Like me, she's half Dutch but with blonde hair instead of black. Well, strawberry blonde. Alright, ginger actually. But she's got legs up to her armpits. And a brazilian. Nearly dropped my metaphorical skateboard, until mum ruined it by telling me that's her spay scar. Urgh, I don't need to hear about girly stuff like that.

My old bachelor pad has been reinstated for her and we've already exchanged a few pleasantries about the weather, mum's driving and so on. I even made her laugh by asking her whether mum ever stopped talking for one minute on the way home. Yes, I approve – so far, at least. I shall call her... Tarquil.

After a lengthy discussion with the oldies, during which mum completely vetoed Tarquil for no good reason, we eventually settled on the name Flicka. As in, 'My Friend Flicka'. I'm assuming that is a subtle hint directed towards me. Whatever. I'm still gonna call her Tarquil anyway.

I have been making Flicka/Tarquil feel welcome by peeing around her bachelorette pad. I think she appreciates the gesture as she's been returning my overtures with some fairly potent scents of her own. That girl sure can waft – I can smell her from my den. Nice. The oldies have been making some rather rude comments about her waft but I don't think they're in any position to preach. Especially the old man, obviously.

I got reacquainted with my old bachelor pad today while Flicka 'The Frenzy' Tarquil ricocheted around the living room. Her old home must have really sucked for her to be *that* excited about living with my oldies. And talk about nosy. I fail to see what is so fascinating about the area behind the TV stand - I've never given it a second glance. And *under* the bookshelves. I think she

---

regretted that one when she emerged covered with dust. Anyway, I had a good poke around her pad and relived some happy memories of stuffed sheep and honking.

Now that her initial manic excitement has worn off slightly, Flicka and I had our first proper chat today and swapped basic life histories. She claims she escaped from 'prison' (a hutch, presumably) and lived rough for a while before the authorities picked her up and put her in the adoption centre. I have my suspicions about her escape story, mostly centred around the fact that the hutch door doesn't appear to have been locked. Or even closed, for that matter. And she is... how do I put this politely... quite a handful. I'm awfully glad she did 'escape' though.

Gave Flicka half my herb ration today. The fact that she actually appreciated the magnitude of this generosity bodes well for our future relationship. Feeling quite happy.

Have that annoying John Barrowman "I made it through the rain" song droning on in my head. Probably because the old man keeps singing it. He's gonna get a punch in the mouth if he doesn't shut up soon.

Is there anything more embarrassing than being chaperoned on a date? And a date in a *bathroom*, moreover? It's so cringe worthy I can hardly bring myself to write about it. Flicka and I spent most of the time avoiding eye contact with each other and nibbling politely on a bit of hay. If my past experience with dating Miss Daisy is anything to go by, I have at least another three of four of these bathroom dates to look forward to. Oh joy.

Still sleeping with the oldies, more or less. Have decided to conduct an experiment on how much sleep they really need – they're on about 5 hours a night now, I reckon, and just beginning to show signs of stress. I'll aim to get them down to 4 hours. Will give them more time to attend to my needs. And Flicka's needs – that girl is really quite demanding. Another reason why I'm still sleeping with the oldies – I don't enjoy listening to her rattling the bars of her cage all night.

Went back to Harley Street again. The old bulgy eye is no better, no worse. The good news is that there's no point carrying on with the eye drops. Although I shall miss the epic battles with the oldies in a strange way. The bad news is that I'll lose the sight in that eye (big deal, I've got another one) and I may need an operation in the future. But that's the future. Right now, I have a hot blonde to attend to.

Longer date with Flicka today, in the oldies bedroom which is an improvement on the bathroom at least. Went rather well, all things considered, although getting stuck in a tunnel is probably not a smooth move when trying to impress a girl. Had to be extricated by mum, with much poorly stifled giggling. Not cool, Bunster. Flicka, bless her heart, pretended not to notice. Starting to feel moderately fond of her.

Flicka is a bit of a dirty girl. I love it. Second 'bedroom date' and I was giving her the obligatory 'I'm the boss' hump, properly nailing her to the floor. She just lay there, loving it. Could it be that the stud muffin has met his match? Quite a worrying thought, actually. I'm not sure the oldies can handle two of us. They feel inferior enough in that department as it is.

Big news today. I have decided to give Flicka her 'wings' and allow her to live with me full time. This was not a decision I took lightly and I was rather persuaded into it by the oldies begging me to let her out. I think the cage rattling has taken its toll on them too. Anyway, the bachelor / bachelorette pad has been stowed away wherever it lives when it's off duty, and Flicka and I are officially cohabiting. I haven't let her in the den yet, of course. She's trying out some new dens of her own. Her favourite seems to be on top of a cardboard box by the kitchen door. Strange girl but hey, whatever makes her happy.

It occurred to me that I am now 'senior bun' and should probably be setting a good example. This is a lot of responsibility but I'm up to it. Miss Daisy trained me well.

I told Flicka about the 'senior bun' thing, puffing out my chest a little and looking as manly as possible (which is extremely manly, I am The Bunster after all). But she didn't look that impressed, to be honest. Truth be told, she looked down her long nose at me and snorted. I should have known. Not only is she a girl, she's a *Dutch* girl. Maybe I'll settle for equals. Maybe.

I am wondering if there is anywhere yet where Flicka *hasn't* been. Inside the washing machine, possibly, although even that wouldn't surprise me. Who does she think she is - Ranulph Fiennes? Next thing she'll be planting flags on every surface she's occupied, like the windowsill and the second shelf of the bookcase. The third shelf has eluded her so far due to a tricky overhang, which is unfortunate as that is where all the food is. Although who needs flags when you have teeth? There are 'Flick Bites' on everything.

Flicka has a lot to learn about living with the oldies. Like, the fact that they are really clumsy. This morning she innocently ran in front of mum as she was walking, sending her flying into the bookcase. Once I'd finished chortling, this reminded me of another family legend. This one was before my time and told to me by Miss Daisy, with much giggling.

Family Legend No 8: The Falling

On one of the oldies' very rare evening excursions, they returned home in a somewhat inebriated state. For some reason, mum thought it would be a good idea to stand on a stool, forgetting that she was wearing a tight skirt. How she got up there is a mystery, how she got down again is self explanatory. Miss Daisy said she was surprised the floorboards didn't break and that she and Whisky laughed for three days straight over it. Wish I'd been there for that one, I must admit.

The oldies have dug out all Miss Daisy's old toys in a desperate and deluded attempt to reduce the Flick Bites on the furniture. Now all the toys have Flick Bites too and the rate of new Flick Bites on the furniture has not diminished at all. Well done, oldies – that was really clever. And why does she get all *my* toys too? My wooden mushroom set is looking decidedly raggedy. I was very fond of that. Granted, I rarely played with it but I did enjoy looking at it.

We just had our first snuggle in the den. Flicka said afterwards that I'm the best she's ever had. Well, duh. The Bunster strikes again. Although this was somewhat spoiled by the fact that I later overheard her telling the old man that I'm the *first* she's ever had. He seemed to think this was rather sweet. I, on the other hand, think it's just plain awesome. I can mould her in my own image.

Honestly, you invite a girl into your den for a snuggle and the next thing you know she's trying to hump you. I don't think so, love – I'm still the boss. Had to put my foot down very firmly. And ignore the giggling as she ran off to tell mum. No respect, these young 'uns.

It is my birthday, apparently. About time too. Conversation with mum this morning went something like this:

Mum: "It's your birthday, Bunster"

Me: "Correction. It's my adoption day"

Mum: "Same thing"

Me: "Well, no it's not actually"

Mum: "You still get presents, don't you?"

Me: "Yes, but no *cake*. See? No *CAKE*"

Mum: "You shouldn't eat cake anyway"

Me: "Are you calling me fat? That's not a very nice thing to say on my birthday..."

I let Flicka open all my presents and very kindly donated all the toys to the 'Anti Flick Bite Fund'. I kept the herbs, obviously. They went straight into my secret stash. Good day.

Flicka is quite obsessed with Long Bailey. She visits him by the door on a regular basis, rubs her chin on his ears and licks his nose. I think she could be grooming him as a potential ally. Dream on darling, us boys always stick together. Long Bailey is *my* buddy.

I'm starting to wonder whether Flicka has batteries. And if so, whether they can be removed. She makes me tired just watching her. Although I must admit, she is an excellent recruit to the sleep deprivation experiment. The manic hallway sprints, the handbrake turns, the honking – all very difficult for the oldies to sleep through. *And* she's continuing Miss Daisy's pioneering work on the pile of magazines under the bed. I'm really rather quite proud of her. Oldies are down to about 4.5 hours sleep a night.

Thought for the day: Now that I am 4 years old (more or less) and this equates to about 40 years old in human terms, I am therefore now officially older than the oldies themselves. I believe this gives me a licence to boss them around and dispense wise words of wisdom at every opportunity. Not that I haven't been doing that anyway, but now I can do it *officially*. Excellent. I can also have a midlife crisis and demand a sports car. I've already got the hot young blonde.

Mum and I took Flicka to the doc today for her first physical. Turns out she has ear mites. Eugh. If I'd known that I never would have snuggled with her. Led to a rather awkward conversation in the car on the way home:

Me: "So, ear mites huh?"

Mum: "Sorry Bailey"

Me: "Didn't think of checking that before you let me snuggle with her?"

Mum: "Like I said, I'm sorry"

Me: "Sorry ain't gonna cut it, sweetheart"

Mum: "I know. There's a banana at home with your name on it"

Me: "*All* bananas have my name on them. What else you got?"

Mum: "Raisins? Cavolo nero? Extra herbs?"

Me: "Yeah, keep talking..."

Flicka hung her head throughout this conversation and pretended to be asleep. Poor girl, it's really not her fault. It's entirely mum's fault.

Both mum and the doc faithfully promised me that the ear mite medicine is no big deal. As I suspected, they both lied. Putting gloop on the nape of my neck is most definitely a big deal. My furs will be messed up for days. *And* I was planning to start my spring moult soon. Might have to delay it a while. How inconvenient.

It's Valentine's Day today, apparently. Oldies are displaying some sickening PDAs again and Flicka keeps looking at me with hopeful eyes. I know my duty and will shortly be taking her to the den for a good snuggle. In private. Valentine's Day, Bunster style.

Auntie B and her little human, Cousin Em, have come to stay for the night. And Mitch, of course. Flicka is thoroughly overexcited and can't sit still for longer than 2 seconds, but she is also too shy to go and socialise. The end result of which is that I now have 'Flicka on speed' bouncing around the den while I'm trying to have a peaceful snooze. Might go and sleep with Mitch instead. That lad knows how to chill.

The oldies are scratching their heads and wondering how in the space of a few hours I managed to get poo stuck to my left ear so bad they had to wash it off. With much retching and giggling, I might add. Very undignified for all involved. Flick and I are saying nothing. What we do in the privacy of the den is our own business and if I want to put my head in her bottom, that's between us. We are both consenting adults, after all.

Thought for the day: Is it possible to be species confused? Flicka spends so much time on her back legs I'm starting to wonder if she really thinks she's a kangaroo. She's certainly got the legs for it. Massive great things. No wonder she can jump so high. Perhaps she could come to the Olympics with me and try out for the high jump. Although that would rather cramp my style at the Olympic village. I hear that place is a hotbed of action, if you know what I mean.

The oldies are still being very rude about Flicka's waft. Personally, I think it's brilliant. The old man has finally met his match in the smell department. I especially like it when she sits right by his feet and wafts. You'd think he wouldn't be able to smell it over his own toxic scent but judging by the vociferous complaints, he smells it alright. Good girl Flicka.

Another trip to the docs with Flicka. Happy to report that the ear mites have been vanquished. In other news, she has put on half a kilo and is now 3kg. Blimey, that's big. And it's not even fat - just pure, solid, rippling muscle. It's lucky she's completely in my thrall - I don't fancy having a fight with *that*. I don't think the old doc fancies it either, he appears to be terrified of her. Probably cos she snorts in disgust whenever he touches her and is like a coiled spring ready to leap. Excellent. Gave her a good snuggling on the way home.

SPRING

Flicka's first nail trimming went fantastically well, from my perspective at least. After an epic battle lasting approximately 20 minutes, Flicka emerged with shorter nails and her dignity intact. The old man, on the other hand, emerged with a bloody nose. Flick's the winner for sure – no contest. What a woman. I'm not sure how she managed to kick him in the face but I am mighty impressed – I've been trying to do that for years. My own nail trimming was accompanied by the usual 'fat' jokes. Boring.

Bailey Bunster's Budget Announcement:

"A recent review of the finances has highlighted a major shortfall and this has left me with no option but to introduce a new "Herb Supply Tax" of 10p in every £1 you earn"

This announcement has been on display under the blankets in the den for several days now so presumably the oldies have both read it. I'm planning to collect the new tax at source from the littering of coins around the place. Considering how little they earn, this will probably only allow me to buy one bag of herbs a month. I can't get too tough on them though. We are in a recession, after all.

Flicka and I have been comparing tail sizes. Happy to report that although she is somewhat larger than me in stature (my short legs have let me down again) my tail is considerably larger than hers. And as we all know, that is the only measurement that truly matters. I reckon my tails accounts for about a fifth of my body weight. Hers is barely a tenth. Still very cute though. Like a little cotton wool ball.

I've spent the last half hour comforting a trembling, traumatised Flicka under the oldies' bed. Yeah, I probably should have warned her to stay away from the bathroom door. Mum has a nasty habit of stepping out of there completely naked. I myself always look the other way when passing the 'danger zone'. Poor Flick's still under the bed, muttering to herself "Why? Why don't they have fur? Why??". I wish I knew the answer.

Flicka's trail of destruction continues. So far, 1 shelf of books (lightly nibbled), 3 rubber doorstops (mangled), mum's Wii Fit elastic band thingy (no great loss, never used) and, my personal favourite, 3 notches in the oldies' bedpost. Gotta be a personal record for them.

Seems the oldies have finally made use of their tiny amount of brain cells and found an antidote to 'Flick Bites'. This comes in the form of a cardboard tunnel covered with hay. Flicka is now as happy as the proverbial pig. I've been fondly observing her and having a little nibble myself now and then. These hay roll things are really quite ingenious. As an added bonus, the entire carpet is now covered with a thin layer of hay, which should wind mum up nicely.

The old bulgy eye is annoying me a bit now. I can't see jack out of it. I ran headfirst into the coffee table this morning. Most embarrassing. In my defence, some idiot (the old man, probably) had moved it several inches from its usual position. He's gonna get a good kicking if he does that again.

I do believe Mothering Sunday should be renamed Smothering Sunday. Mum's been following me around like a lovelorn puppy all day. I finally took pity on her and allowed her to kiss me on the nose but made it clear that's her lot for the year. No more kisses. Not even on the bottom. Although she probably does that anyway while I'm sleeping. Talk about taking advantage.

Due no doubt in part to the 'coffee table incident', mum escorted me back to Harley Street today. Hannibal Lecter tutted and fussed for a little while and then told us to come back again in a month or so. Well done mum, another brilliant waste of time.

Can't work out whether Flicka is a blithering idiot or a ginger genius. Example – conversation she had with mum this morning. Although calling it a 'conversation' is probably giving it a status it doesn't deserve.

Mum: "Flicka-licka-licka-licka!"

Flicka: (jumping in the air) "Yeah yeah yeah yeah!"

Mum: "Flicka-licka-licka-licka-licka-licka-licka!!"

Flicka: (180 degree turn midair) "Yeah yeah yeah yeah yeah yeah yeah!!"

Whereupon she was presented with a morsel of dried pineapple. OK, so she got the goods but it seems like an awful lot of effort was involved. I myself can get a pineapple chunk out of mum with the simple expedient of a steely glare. I guess I am senior bun after all. Result.

Spent most of the day snuggled in the den with my nose buried in Flicka's soft white tummy while she groomed my ears and back. Seems a bit too good to be true. Briefly wondered if I'd died in my sleep and gone to heaven, but then remembered that the oldies are still here so that's not very likely. Now I am wondering if this is just karma, pure and simple. I did spend a *lot* of time grooming Miss Daisy, not that I minded. Every silver lining has a cloud though – I may be getting good lovin' from Flick but I still have to return the favour. And she's *huge*. My poor tongue.

How exactly Flicka got a piece of sticky tape stuck to her tail is a mystery to me, but she was a brave girl while the oldies removed it and now I have to kiss it better. Poor me. Maybe that will teach her there are some areas you shouldn't venture into, but I doubt it. Come to think of it, she probably did it on purpose to get a tail kissing off me. Ginger genius indeed.

It's taken mum three whole days to do her bookkeeping. Either she is stupid (quite likely) or she spends way too much time admiring me. Either way,

I'm embarrassed for her. She's probably got it wrong anyway.

Thought for the day: If The Bunster doesn't see it happen, does it really happen? This is like that tree-falling-in-the-woods thing and is worth pondering. This morning, for example, I was chilling on the rug, minding my own business. I could hear a gnawing to my left, but I couldn't see it. Therefore, I can't be held responsible (whatever mum says) for the fact that Flicka took several bites out of the bookshelf whilst under my 'supervision'. This senior bun thing does have its downsides – I never signed up to be a nursemaid.

Was doing my laps of the coffee table this morning (Olympics will be here before we know it) when Flicka emerged from the den unawares, causing me to run smack into her ribs. Luckily, she is pretty well padded and neither of us were hurt. It did make me think though, she's let herself go a bit. Maybe I won't be the sole recipient of the fat jokes for much longer.

Flicka is a worse honker than me. She honks all the time, everywhere she goes, for no reason whatsoever that I can make out. Often it is accompanied by a good wafting. Starting to feel really very fond of her now.

The blonde bombshell delivered a perfect one-inch paw punch deep into mum's belly button this morning, ending her lazy lie-in. Starting to wonder if she's actually a trained assassin sent by the government to ensure Bailey Bunster gets his brekkie on time. Codename: 'Ginga Ninja', perhaps. The perfect foil to my 007.

Easter already. Time flies when you're having fun, I guess. I've never really understood the whole 'Easter Bunny' thing. For one thing, we don't lay eggs. And as for being a symbol of rebirth the chances of that are pretty slim, thank goodness. I shudder at the thought of a lot of little Flickas running around the place. The best thing about Easter, in my opinion, is the appearance of the Cadbury's Caramel Bunny on TV. That girl is smokin' hot. And the voice – wow. Now that I think about it, Flicka does bear a certain resemblance to her – maybe I'll ask her to put a ribbon round her neck and talk softly to me about chocolate.

On my foragings today I found a box designed to hold six Cadburys Crème Eggs. Regrettably, it was full of apple twigs instead of crème eggs. Now, either Cadburys have pulled a fast one, or mum has eaten six eggs all by herself *already*. What a pig. She could have saved me *one*, at the very least.

Mum has just informed me that she will be doing something called 'work' this week. This is a very rare occurrence and is some cause for concern. Especially when she added that she will be going *out* to do this 'work'. All day, every day, for a whole week. Unacceptable. I am used to her popping in and out, of course, but to leave me alone all day is bang out of order. The old man rarely leaves his study and is completely incapable of attending to my needs properly. As for Flicka, she's more of a liability than a help to anyone.

Day 2 of the 'work week' and I am already feeling extremely neglected. Where are my regular hay top ups? My herb rations? My afternoon snuggle? Grumpy Bunster.

So not only am I being neglected, I am now being scolded. Conversation with mum this evening on her return from 'work':

Mum: "Hey Bails, ok? I missed you"

Me: "Herbs, please"

Mum: "In a minute, let me get my coat off"

Me: "Now. Herbs. Now"

Mum: (dishing out herbs) "Ummm Bailey, what happened to that book?"

Me: (munching) "Dunno. Flick chewed it"

Mum: "You're supposed to be watching her!"

Me: "Correction. *You* are supposed to be watching her. *You* adopted her, not me"

Mum: "But I have to work..."

Me: "Not my problem"

Honestly, do I have to do everything around here? Hopefully the 'Bookgate' incident will at least put an end to this work nonsense and get mum back where she belongs. Here, waiting on me hand and foot. A suspicious mind might even think I put Flick up to it, but that would just be cruel. It *was* one of mum's favourite books, after all.

I fear a bedroom ban is imminent. Ricocheting off the bedroom walls at 5am is probably pushing the envelope of the oldies' tolerance. Needless to say, it was the Ginga Ninja doing the ricocheting, not me. My style is more of a gentle cardboard nibbling. It's surprising how easily that wakes them up with very little effort involved.

It occurred to me today that the old man's study has been off limits since Miss Daisy left. There are two possible reasons for this, I think. (1) he's got so much crap in there now that you can't actually get in the door, or (2) the Council have finally got round to declaring it as a public health hazard and blocked it off for good. Anyway, it reminded me of another family legend.

Family Legend No 9: The Nibbling

Back in the day when Whisky and Miss Daisy ruled the roost, the oldies returned home one day to find no sign of them anywhere. They looked high and low with rising panic, before it dawned on one of them to look in the study. Whereupon they discovered Whisky and Miss

Daisy whistling innocently, surrounded by speaker cables cut neatly into 10cm lengths. I'm not sure who did the breaking and entering, although I suspect Miss Daisy, but I think it's safe to say they both participated in the cable carnage. All hail to them – my heroes.

Played 'dead Bailey' with the oldies this evening. I'm only able to do this once or twice a year, otherwise it wouldn't work. One minute I'm sitting on the rug as usual, the next I'm flat on my side and the oldies are on the edge of the sofa in panic, poised to call 999 and give me mouth-to-mouth. I try and hold my breath for a bit to give a genuine impression of imminent death. Then comes the coup de grace – a casual flap of the ear, sending the oldies sinking back into the sofa in relief. I love this game, it really makes them appreciate me. It's always swiftly followed by a generous herb ration and a cuddle. Good times.

Thought for the day: it's the little things in life that bring happiness. Like today, for example, when mum stepped on a squidger and trod it all over the place before realising. Slippers went in the washing machine, complete with that elusive toggle. Really must get around to swiping that. Need a good plan.

After a night of complicated planning and general strategery, I executed a rather impressive lightning strike on the slipper toggle as mum emerged unawares from the bathroom in the dim morning light. Told you it would be mine. Happy day.

Auntie B and Mitch have come to stay for the weekend. The oldies and I are both rather hoping that Flick will choose to sleep in her bedroom, not ours, but as she still goes all shy around her this is looking rather unlikely. I don't know what she's scared of, Auntie B is well cool. She gave me a nice little back scratch when she arrived, before mum dragged her into the kitchen for another of their interminable chats. What *do* they talk about? Me, probably.

Oldies have so far held off on a complete bedroom ban, which I think is wise of them. This morning when they kicked us out at about 5am Flicka went and cut off their internet connection, leading to much oldie annoyance when they finally stumbled out of their pit. Order is restored – we always win. They're so naïve though – they reckon Flick doesn't do it deliberately and that she just has an 'extremely low boredom threshold'. That's putting it mildly.

The Flick Bites continue. It's getting hard to see the furniture for all the Bites, in fact. And I'm starting to wonder if Flicka's long-term aim is actually to completely destroy all the furniture and make the oldies live on the floor like us. Intriguing concept, but they'd better not try and get in the den with us. Some things are sacred.

Hell hath no fury like a Flicka shut out of the bedroom. Furniture moved, toys thrown, and Ken Hom lying mangled on the floor (the cookbook, not the man). Low boredom threshold indeed. She's just a psycho, pure and simple. Beautiful psycho, though.

Thought for the day: I don't ask much of my oldies, just their constant undivided attention and servitude, and in return they get the honour of living with me. It hardly seems fair. But that's life, I suppose. We all have our crosses to bear.

Mum's been bouncing around all day with a big smile on her face. When I finally gave in and asked her what was so exciting, she produced the Sunday Times newspaper with a flourish and said "Look, your name's in the paper!" Was momentarily excited (and a little worried – who knows what dirt the Sunday Times could have found on me?) before realising that the stupid article was all about *rabbits*. What's that got to do with me? I'd forgotten all about mum's silly Bunnyhugga website. She is very happy though. I don't think we'll be getting *that* particular newspaper in our litter trays, that's for sure.

Flicka's going through a hay roll every week or so. That's a serious habit she's got there. And that's just the big ones – she's got umpteen little ones on the go as well. *And* a nasty habit of leaving them in my running routes so I smack into them head first. Very amusing, I'm sure. When I complained she told me not be such a wuss. The cheek of it. The Bunster is *not* a wuss. I'm hard as nails.

After two or more years of playing the same song every Thursday night, the band in the church next door have finally picked a new one to try. They are currently playing "Nearer My God to Thee". Very badly, with bagpipes. I feel like I'm on the Titanic with half a dozen drowning cats. And I never got those earplugs I wanted for Christmas, unfortunately. I'll just have to shove my head in Flicka's tummy. You can't hear a thing when you're in there. And it's lovely and wafty.

Speaking of the Titanic, and Flicka's tummy, she is mighty fond of rolling on her back in a coquettish manner and looking at me lovingly from under her long eyelashes. I suspect she wants me to 'draw her like one of my French girls'. If she had The Heart of the Ocean around her neck, I might consider it. What *really* pops into my head when she does this is: Iceberg, dead ahead. I don't tell her that, of course.

I have just been informed that the oldies are going *out*. In the *evening*. This is so rare I can hardly remember the last time it happened. My initial outrage has been mollified somewhat by the offer of an early dinner and sole ownership of the remote control. I might put on Watership Down and give Flick nightmares.

That'll teach me. Flick's been singing 'Bright Eyes' all day long. It's doing my head in.

Went back to Harley Street with mum today. I fear the day of reckoning is upon us and Hannibal Lecter is itching to get his hands on my dodgy eye. He must have got hold of a nice Chianti after all. Had an annoying and pointless conversation with mum in the car on the way home:

Mum: "Bit scary, isn't it Bunster?"

Me: "What, your driving? I couldn't agree more... did you even *see* that cyclist?"

Mum: "No, silly... the eye operation"

Me: "Oh that... nah, it'll be a doddle"

Mum: "Promise you'll be ok, Bails?"

Me: "Well, I can't promise that... old Dr Lecter might decide he wants my liver too"

Mum: (shivering) "Don't say that... he's very nice, you know"

Me: (darkly) "Yeah... time will tell"

The end result of which is that she now has her knickers completely in a twist about the whole thing. And when we got home she promptly transferred her fear to the old man and now he's a freaked out mess *too*. On the upside, I should at least get some extra herbage out of it.

I was correct about the herbage. Excellent ration today. I have another week of this to look forward to. Gonna milk it for all it's worth, obviously. Should be good for a couple of bananas too.

So, diary – the big day is here. Today I am off to Harley Street for what one hopes will be the final time. Wish me luck. No doubt the oldies will spend the whole day pacing and wringing their hands. I should jolly well think so too. I've left Long Bailey in charge of Flicka and the oldies and if I don't come back I expect you to initiate the diary self-destruct sequence. Keep my secrets safe, please.

Hello diary. Well, I made it. Sorry I didn't say hello last night but man, those were some serious drugs I was on. I was off my head, seeing unicorns and pink rabbits and green fairies. I swear at one point I saw Andy Murray getting into the Wimbledon final. Freaky stuff. Must be what LSD feels like. I also vaguely remember the old man holding me steady as I was staggering around coming down from my trip. Was rather comforting. Damn him. If he's expecting gratitude, he'll be waiting a long time.

[later] Still feeling sick as a dog. Spent most of the day in my litter tray, with my head resting pitifully on the edge while mum fussed anxiously around me. Flicka is being blisteringly unsympathetic, merely flying in now and then to nudge me bossily and tell me to hurry up and get better. Woe is me.

Feeling much better today. But worryingly, the oldies inform me that Andy Murray *did* get into the Wimbledon final. Are they winding me up? And more importantly, does this mean that the unicorns and pink rabbits were real??

Me and the missus have been having some relationship issues. Flicka claims that in my delirium I transferred ownership of the den to her. I find this highly unlikely but rather than argue the point I am now engaged in a series of stealth tactics to re-take the den. It will be mine, oh yes it will.

Was fully expecting the old bulgy eye to be returned to me in a glass jar, but mum tells me it's been 'sent to the lab for testing'. Yeah, right. I imagine it is currently residing on a dinner plate next to some fava beans, perhaps with a sprig of parsley on top, while the fine doctor uncorks his Chianti. How disappointing. It would have made an excellent Halloween prop.

The northern end of the den is now under my control. Flicka still controls the southern end. She has been making friendly overtures for several hours now, so I expect full Bunster control will be resumed by morning.

I think Flicka has learned a valuable lesson today. Namely, Bailey always wins. As predicted, the den is now back in the hands of its rightful owner (me) *and* I took her to the bedroom for a snuggle under the oldies' bed. For 10 *whole minutes*. That's right, blondie - Bunster got his mojo back.

Feeling rather perky. The old bulgy eye must have been troubling me more than I realised. I've even started to 'play' again. Good grief. There's life in the old Bunster yet. Well, someone's gotta keep Flick occupied and the oldies are always pleading 'work'. That's my excuse, anyway. Can't let the oldies think I'm happy or anything like that. They'll backslide straight away into pure laziness.

Have been trying out my pirate impressions. Got the old 'aaaaargggghhhh' and 'shiver me timbers' off pat but really it doesn't work without a parrot on my shoulder. Will have to put that on my Christmas list. 1 x green parrot. I shall name it... Tarquil.

Caught Flicka trying to nibble off Long Bailey's left eye. Poor chap. She claims she was just trying to help and that he wants to look like me, but I think in truth she just wanted his eye. Those wooden buttons are a constant temptation to her. She has a bit of a wood fetish, I think. And rubber. And clothing. Well, everything really.

Despite Flicka's many faults, she does have *some* redeeming qualities. Like when she wraps herself around me in the den so I'm spooned on three sides and snug as a bug. I think she's trying to tell me I'm *her* Bunster now. Bit presumptuous but ok. I can live with that.

Conversation overheard between Flicka and the old man this evening while I was snoozing in the den:

Old man: "Flick, did you just waft?"

Flicka: (smirking) "Nah, must have been you"

Old man: (choking) "That's disgusting"

Flicka: "You love it!"

Old man: "I do not love it"

Flicka: "You love me though, don't you?"

Old man: "In spite of the waft, yes"

Flicka: (smugly) "Yeah, s'cos I'm gorgeous, innit?"

Old man: "Yup"

Nice to see the old man being put in his place by a female again. Mum is pathetically inadequate in that respect. She's actually quite nice to him most of the time.

After months of being terrorised by 'The Flick-Knife', the oldies say they've finally had enough and are 'putting the foot down'. Should be jolly good entertainment; or better than the TV, at least. I'm not sure what 'putting the foot down' consists of exactly, but whatever it is I'm sure Flicka has the answer to it. And then some.

So much for putting the foot down. Flicka gets more spoiled by the day. She's somehow managed to start a new tradition – the 'after-midnight-carrot-and-before-bedtime' treat. This means she races through her carrot while the oldies are doing whatever they do in the bathroom, then races to their bedroom, leaps onto the bed and bounces around for several minutes looking cute until they give her a treat. I disapprove, in theory, but as mum always sneaks me a raisin or three on her way to bed I can't complain too much. And at least my dignity is intact. Flicka has no shame.

Thought for the day: If the oldies bought me all the herbs in the world and piled them up in a mountain, how big would it be? Bigger than Everest? Quite possibly. Would it be enough to keep me 'herb happy' for the rest of my life? Doubtful.

The oldies and I have bestowed a new nickname on Flicka. Namely, 'Skidmark'. This is due to the fact that she goes everywhere at a breakneck pace which is not entirely compatible with slippery laminate floors. Oldies think it's hilarious, but then they are very easily entertained. I think it's just mildly entertaining. And when she skids into *me*, just plain painful.

While I was inspecting Flicka's huge nuts by the litter tray today, I had a brilliant idea for a home business. They would make an excellent plant fertiliser. All I have to do is get mum to sweep them up into a jar, screw the top on tight and stick it on Ebay. I shall call it 'Flick Fertiliser'. And I even have a new product in the pipeline, 'Eau de Flicka', although that might be slightly more difficult to collect. I don't fancy following her around with a jar, waiting for the waft. If I could get hold of it though, I'm sure it would fly off the shelves. London, Paris, New York. I'm gonna be a billionaire.

Feeling rather insulted by the patronising way in which the oldies applauded my win of the 'hallway race for brekkie' this morning. Just cos my legs are short, doesn't mean I can't get up a good speed once I get going. They don't call me 'The Bunster Train' for nothing.

[later] Stop press. Half an hour ago Flicka enlarged my 'diary hole' and boldly went where no bun has gone before – *inside* the sofa. Crazy chick. She's bouncing around inside there now, having a whale of a time, while mum hovers anxiously and says stupid things like "Don't hurt yourself!" and "Come out now, please Flick!". Once she emerges, the oldies will no doubt block the hole up for good so regrettably I think that the time has come to say goodbye to you, diary.

It's been a wild ride and I'll miss you but all good things must come to an end. Perhaps Flicka or some other enterprising young blood will discover you one day, dust you off and carry on. Or maybe you'll just moulder in the sofa until it finally collapses under the weight of the oldies. I wish you luck, whatever you do. I myself plan to spend the rest of my days lounging against Flicka's white belly, snacking on herbs, insulting the old man and winding mum up. Good times.

Bunster to the Max. Over and out.

Made in the USA
Las Vegas, NV
07 February 2022

43348775R00066